Lá Fhéile Vailintín '25

I love you —

-Séanie

Brehons and Brahmins

Resonances between Irish and Indian cultures

Manchán Magan

Illustrated by
Aurélie Beatley

Brehons and Brahmins

Resonances between Irish and Indian cultures

Manchán Magan

Published in Ireland in 2024 by

Mayo Books Press

Market Street, Castlebar, County Mayo, F23 HN29
www.MayoBooksPress.com

Illustrated by:
Aurélie Beatley

Design and layout:
SiobhanFoody.com

ISBN: 978-1-914596-35-3

CONTENTS

Introduction

Ireland and India seem far apart, with apparently little in common in terms of culture, language, and tradition. Yet appearances can be deceiving: there are, in fact, remarkable similarities between the cultures that, once noticed, are impossible to ignore. They point to a shared kinship thousands of years ago that upends the concept of separation between Eastern and Western cultures.

We are both descendants of the Indo-European peoples who migrated west to Europe and south-east to India from a central area between Russia, Ukraine, and western Kazakhstan thousands of years ago. (Some argue that it was from Asia Minor, now Turkey, that they spread, or Armenia, or maybe even India itself.) These early migrants brought their language and beliefs with them, along with their pioneering new methods of farming.

The early Indo-European language they spoke became the basis for almost all European languages. One significant branch of this early language was proto-Celtic, which by the third century BC was spoken from

Ireland, in the west, through to the central plain of Turkey, in the east. It morphed into a variety of Celtic languages and cultures that over time were eroded by a slew of invading armies and empires passing through mainland Europe. The Greek and Roman empires were particularly influential in eroding Celtic influence and replacing it with Hellenic and Latin culture through much of Europe, but Ireland managed to avoid these outside influences until Christian missionaries began to appear in the fifth century AD.

Being on the far western margins, Ireland was able to preserve a surprising amount of its early Indo-European culture, and India was able to do likewise on the eastern margins. In Ireland we avoided dilution of the customs, beliefs, and language that had taken root here and so retained aspects of the culture that we had once shared with people on the Indian subcontinent. Think of it as a pebble dropped into a pool that caused circular ripples to radiate out: Ireland and India are like different points on the same ripple.

This book is a gentle meander along the circumference of this ripple, an exploration of aspects of language, mythology, social structure, and legal system that Ireland and India appear to have in common. It is largely based on research by the Celtic scholar Myles Dillon published in *Celts and Aryans* (1973) and on the work of the Welsh social anthropologist Alwyn D. Rees and his brother Brinley, a classics scholar, who together wrote *Celtic Heritage: Ancient Tradition in Ireland and Wales* (1961).

The word 'Aryan' in the title of Dillon's book comes from the Sanskrit *arya*, and Old Irish *aire*, meaning 'noble'. The term Aryan is now somewhat contentious, as it is associated with the baseless, pseudoscientific claims popularised by the Nazis—a toxic and sinister hypothesis according to which Germans are descended from a supposedly superior race of Aryan Nordic people who migrated to India 1,600 years ago. Scholars and historians reject any association between the term Aryan and racist fantasies.

The core concept of true Aryanism is a spiritual state that transcends sectarian notions of race, uniting people by noble and conscious behaviour towards themselves and others, including animals and the environment, while harmonising their lives with the divine. In finding commonalities and connections between Ireland and India today we must steer clear of the lies and misinterpretations that became a cornerstone of Nazism and state clearly that their claims were rooted in racial prejudice and false anthropology. It is time to clear-sightedly take back the true legacy of our Indo-European heritage and not be cowed by Hitler's conniving attempts to appropriate it.

This book is intended to be an exploration rather than a demonstration of any particular truth. I urge you to reflect on the extent to which echoes of an ancient Eurasian culture might still linger in Irish lore. Be assured that, as a lay person without any academic prowess, I have barely scratched the surface of the myriad potential strands that run between our respective cultures. There is much more to be explored in this field, hopefully by those more qualified than me. But it is a start.

But before we dive in I should mention that there is a controversial counter-hypothesis about the migration of people across Europe and Asia. A few outsider academics claim that the movement of culture and people may have been not westwards but eastwards. That survivors of a flood may have landed along the western margins of Ireland, Scotland, France, and Spain and spread their language, culture, and lineage from there across Europe towards Asia. There is not enough evidence to advance this idea at present.

Origin Stories of Ireland and India

L ebor Gabála Érenn ('The Book of Invasions') is a semi-mythological account in poetry and prose of the first five groups of settlers to have occupied Ireland. Its earliest parts can be traced back to the seventh century, though presumably these accounts are based on knowledge that is far older.

The first wave of settlers are said to have been led by Cesair, a granddaughter of Noah from the biblical flood story. The second group are said to be descendants of Noah's and sailed from Greece and Sicily. The stories in *Lebor Gabála Érenn* list other migrant influxes from the Caspian Sea and even from Egypt. Scholars tend to dismiss the whole account as pseudo-history, and clearly there is an attempt to entwine the origins of Ireland with Old Testament texts, but there may be more ancient influences too.

The account provided by *Lebor Gabála Érenn* has strong parallels with the origin story of India as told in the *Rigveda*, the oldest known Vedic Sanskrit text, parts of which date back three or even four thousand years.

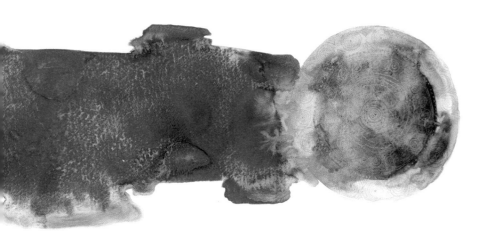

The 'Five Kindreds' section of the *Rigveda* describes five waves of immigrants who settled in India from across the sea. These were not so much invasions as incarnations of spirits into human form, or transportations of beings from one dimension to another. Often, the journey was made by ship or heavenly chariot, just as it was in the Irish tradition when there was a crossing from this world to supernatural worlds such as Tír na nÓg. The 'Five Kindreds' section describes this journey in reverse, from an existence of infinite possibility to a more limited physical manifestation on Earth.

Interestingly, the final wave of settlers to Ireland before the current inhabitants, Tuatha Dé Danann, are said to have arrived in ships or in clouds through the air, which are reminiscent of the *Rigveda*'s heavenly chariots. It is worth bearing in mind that earlier versions of the Irish myths might not have specified the destination from which the settlers arrived and instead said something like 'faraway shores', implying that they came from beyond the physical realm.

Invoking the Land: Amergin and Krishna

The arrival of the current wave of settlers to Ireland was said to have been led by a druidic poet, Amergin, who summoned the world to life by reciting an incantation when he stepped foot on the island for the first time. As well as invoking the world into reality, his words were intended to take possession of it from the semi-divine beings who existed before him. Summoning all things in this world and beyond, he chanted:

I am wind on sea. I am ocean wave. I am roar of sea. I am stag of seven tines. I am hawk on cliff. I am shining tear of sun. I am gentle herbs.

Likewise, the ancient Hindu scripture *Bhagavad Gita* claims that, about five thousand years ago, during the Kurukshetra War, Lord Krishna uttered a declaration claiming the entirety of creation as a manifestation of his energy:

I am the radiant sun among the light-givers ... Among the stars of night, I am the moon ... I am Meru among mountain peaks ... I am the ocean among the waters ... I am the Wind ... Of vibrations, I am the transcendental OM ... Of immovable things, I am the Himalayas ... Of all trees, I am the holy fig tree.

His most famous invocation is 'I am mighty Time, the source of destruction that comes forth to annihilate the worlds.'

रसोऽहमप्सु कौन्तेय प्रभास्मि शशिसूर्ययो: |
प्रणव: सर्ववेदेषु शब्द: खे पौरुषं नृषु || 8||

I am the taste in water, O son of Kunti,
and the radiance of the sun and the moon.
I am the sacred syllable Om in the Vedic mantras;
I am the sound in ether, and the ability in humans.

Both Amergin and Krishna seem to be suggesting that they are the ultimate unifier of all things. They are the creative force at the heart of existence.

Incest in Irish and Indian Mythology

The three supreme gods of Hinduism are Vishnu, Shiva, and Brahma. The latter is less acclaimed but is nevertheless considered a creator god who produced demons, creatures, days and nights, and even other gods from his mind and the various forms that he could shapeshift into. At one point he split his body in two to create the goddess Saraswati, who is associated with rivers and pooling water. Brahma became so enchanted by her that he sprouted four more heads to be able to gaze at her from all directions. This is meant as a cautionary tale about getting too caught up in our own creations. It is also a warning against incest, as Saraswati could be considered a daughter who later became his lover, giving birth to Manu, the first human being.

Incest being part of a culture's foundational myth is common throughout the world, as it was logical to assume that we all sprang from an original 'first' couple, who were probably shaped from a single entity.

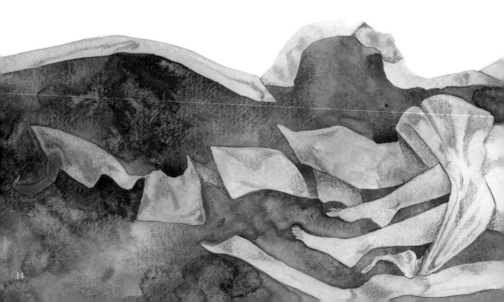

If Ireland had a foundational creation story it has not survived, though there are frequent references to incestuous relationships in the mythology.

It is said that Ireland's current settlers descend from a man called Míl of Spain. His daughter Odba was among the first of our people to land in Ireland and had three children with Étemón, Míl's son. This seems to imply that we, the people of Ireland (known as 'the Sons of Míl'), are the product of incest, just as the people of India ('the Sons of Manu') can also be seen in this light.

In neither culture was incest permitted or encouraged, and accounts of Odba and Saraswati are not emphasised in Irish or Indian lore, although an eminent high king of Irish mythology, Conaire Mór, was the son of Mess Búachalla, who was the product of incest, and new DNA evidence from bones found in the ritual cairn at Newgrange has revealed that Ireland's most esteemed rulers did engage in incest five thousand years ago.

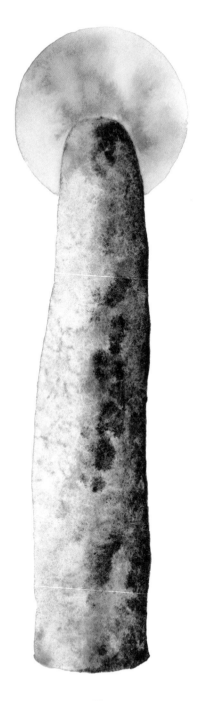

Liath Fáil and Shiva Linga

The Liath Fáil, or Fál, is an ancient coronation stone on the Hill of Tara in Co. Meath that is said to have been brought to Ireland by the godlike race Tuatha Dé Danann. It is reputed to have uttered a shriek or to have sung out when a king willed by destiny sat upon it. It is generally regarded as representing a phallus, as are other tall vertical stones in the landscape. Occasionally, they are in pairs and are known as pillar stones, through which cattle were ritualistically paraded as part of cleansing and strengthening ceremonies.

The Liath Fáil was so important that the Irish defined themselves in relation to it, calling themselves 'men of Fál', who lived on Inis Fáil, ('Island of Fál'). Still today, one of Ireland's principal political parties, Fianna Fáil ('Warriors of Fál'), is named after it.

Ritual stones in the shape of the male sexual organ are a common trope of ancient fertility cults throughout the world, but the tradition appears to have survived strongest, or most evidently, in India, where the Shiva linga, or lingam, a stylised or sculptural representation of Lord Shiva's phallus, is a core component of Hindu temples and shrines. The Shiva linga represents all the energies of this world, and beyond, that are manifested within Lord Shiva.

In non-Hindu traditions within India, phallic forms have also continued to have currency, such as in the state of Rajasthan, where phallic symbols played a central role in the coronation of maharajahs into the mid-twentieth century.

Brehons and Brahmins | *Resonances between Irish and Indian cultures*

Sheela na Gig and Ghee

Ireland and India also had female fertility symbols. The most conspicuous in Ireland are the figurative carvings of naked women displaying an exaggerated vulva known as Sheela na Gigs. These stone sculptures date from the Middle Ages but appear to be remnants of some earlier ritualistic totem figure that may have been carved in wood or moulded in clay. The word Sheela could refer to *sí* ('fairy') or *silleadh* ('to drip', 'to pour') or be a general name for a woman. The word na implies the genitive case ('of the'). The nearest Irish words to *gig* are *gcíoch* ('of the breasts') and *gaoth* (pronounced 'gee', meaning 'wind').

In connection with India, what comes to mind is the Sanskrit word *śileya* ('stone'), which is interesting considering that Sheela na Gigs are carved in stone, and the word ghee, the clarified yak or buffalo butter used as a sacred ointment in Hindu and Buddhist rituals. In Hindu religious practice, ghee represents the feminine life force and the ability to generate. Women in India still today rub ghee into certain statues to aid their fertility. Melted ghee is poured on the lingam in a ritual to symbolise and support the fertility of the land, animals, plants, and humans.

This association between butter and women's health was also to be found in Ireland, where butter was used by healers and holy women to aid in gynaecological matters and other health issues. In fact, there's the proverb 'Whatever butter or whiskey can't cure cannot be cured.' Some Sheela na Gigs appear to have an oily, ghee-like substance oozing from their genitals, such as the one on Ballinderry Castle in Co. Galway, which brings to mind the fact that a common slang word in Ireland for the vagina is 'gee'. There may be some connection there, though it is vague or tenuous at present.

Is the Prime Goddess of Ireland Indian?

Among the inhabitants of Ireland before the current settlers were Tuatha Dé Danann, a supernatural tribe of earthbound gods who inhabited Ireland before we settled here, according to legend. They were descendants of the god Dagda, who in turn was descended from the Mother Earth figure Anu (alternatively Áine or d'Anu). Anu was an ancient river goddess throughout Europe and is thought to be the same god that Hindus worship as Danu or Ama.

Ancient Hindu texts refer to a race called the Dānavas, who were the sons of Danu, and in Hindu cosmology Danu is connected with the waters of heaven. Could the Dānavas and Tuatha Dé Danann be the same people?

Interestingly, the Dānavas are known for their technical prowess. One of their kings, Māyā Danava, was a noted architect and engineer who designed and built a futuristic city in Sri Lanka and a palace in India that had within it both natural and 'magical' ponds and lakes. This technical ability chimes with the sophisticated flying ships in which Tuatha Dé Danann were said to have arrived in Ireland and also with the fact that the Tuatha Dé Danann king Nuada had a prosthetic arm made of silver engineered for him.

In both Pagan Ireland and Vedic India the soil was considered the residence of the divinity and was worshipped as the body of the Goddess, and many geographical features were thought to be her physical features. In both countries the land was seen as pulsating with life and connected with other realms at significant points. In Hindi these points are known as *tirthas*, meaning fords or crossing places between different worlds, which are still regularly visited on pilgrimages. In Irish the equivalent term is *tairsigh*, meaning thresholds, boundaries, or entranceways into buildings or into other worlds.

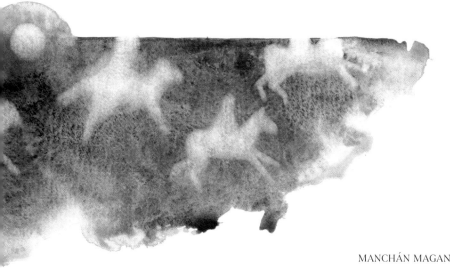

Druids and Brahmins

T he druids in Ireland were thought to have been descendants of Tuatha Dé Danann, or at least to have been in communication with them. They were responsible for the preservation of the collective memory of the tribe. The Irish for druid is *draoi*, and its genitive form in Old Irish was *druad*.

The word appears to stem from two Proto-Celtic words whose roots have parallels in Sanskrit, *dru* and *vid*. In the earliest forms of Irish the word *dru* meant 'immersion' or 'total connection'. It also referred to the oak, specifically to a sacred tree of life whose central trunk ran through the middle of the cosmos. In India this central trunk, or world axis, was called *dhruva*.

Vid, *weyd*, or *oid* meant 'knowledge', 'observation', or 'taking heed' in Proto-Celtic. Oideas means 'knowledge' in Modern Irish, and in Sanskrit the closely related word *veda* means the same thing. So, a druid was one immersed in knowledge.

That said, etymology is a notoriously complex discipline, and a case has been made for the Irish word *draoi* and its English derivation, druid, having a common root in the Hindi *drishti*, meaning 'focused gaze', and the Sanskrit *rishi*, meaning 'seer'.

In Indian society the role of the druid was held by Brahmins. As in Ireland, this figure represented the religious and learned class of society. The Celtic druid and Brahmin priest shared a belief that memory was the life-giving and sustaining power of the universe. They both appear to have been more powerful than kings, as seen in 'The Tale of Briciú's Feast', in which it is Sencha the druid who tells the king to separate the fighting warriors, and in *Táin Bó Cuailnge* ('The Cattle Raid of Cooley'), which makes it clear that the king may not speak until the druid has spoken.

Poetry and Magic

The arrival of Christian missionaries in the fifth century led to the end of the druids' reign. Their spiritual role was usurped by monks and missionaries, and their role as guardians of history and genealogy was taken over by the *filí* ('poets'). A similar duality developed in Indian bardic tradition, with a tension between practitioners of religious and secular verse. The *dan-stuti* was composed by the *brahmarsi* ('Brahmin priest-poet'), while the *narasamsi* was composed by the *rajarsi* ('warrior-poet'). The equivalent of the *rajarsi* in Irish is *rigfilis* ('king-poet').

The term *rajarsi* stems from *raja* ('king'), and this same word gave us the Irish word *rí* ('king'). A raja ruled with the help of local Brahmin judges, just as a rí ruled with the assistance of Brehon judges, who were the lawyers of Ireland. Their laws, known as Brehon Law, contain numerous parallels with India's Lawbook of Manu. The word 'Brehon' is an anglicisation of the Irish word for judge, *breitheamh*, which stems from the Old Irish *breth* ('carrier of' and 'judgments'). The Indo-European root word was *berrih* which is also the derivation of the Hindi word Brahmin. *Breth/Berrih* could be translated as 'keeper of mantras'.

St Moling and Vishnu

While St Moling was training to be a priest in Co. Carlow in the seventh century, he set out on a long walk to practise austerities by collecting alms with nothing but a begging bowl, two wallets, and a staff of ash wood. An evil spectre and his demonic mob accosted him, threatening to stab him with a sword. St Moling responded by declaring that he would batter him with his staff. It was a stalemate. By way of resolution, St Moling asked as a favour whether he could take three single steps towards heaven. The spectre granted the request. St Moling's first hop was no larger than that of a crow on a hilltop. His second leap took him out of sight entirely, and on the third one he landed on the wall of a monastery. The spectre and his mob gave chase, but he was safely within the walls of the church by then.

A similar story is told about Vishnu, one of the three supreme gods of Hinduism. While he was on retreat in a hermitage, practising meditation, he was asked by Indra and some other gods to confront the demon Bali, who was performing evil sacrifices. Vishnu agreed, and after disguising himself as a short-legged dwarf, he begged Bali to be allowed to take three steps. The request was granted, and Vishnu transformed himself into a long-legged, monstrous creature able to take a leap that encompassed the whole Earth, which he did. His second leap spanned the entire atmosphere, and the third traversed the sky. He then cast Bali to the underworld and bequeathed these three worlds to the god Indra.

Vishnu's soubriquet, the 'thrice-stepper', arose from this incident, just as St Moling's name derives from the verb *ling*, meaning 'to leap' or 'to attack'. In place of St Moling's sacred ash stick, Vishnu carried a *kaumodaki* ('mace', a generic term for a weapon that could fend off a spiritual threat). The St Moling story dates from the time of his early life, about AD 640, while Vishnu's tale is recorded in the two-thousand-year-old *Ramayana*, with earlier versions in the far older *Shatapatha Brahmana*.

Classes and Castes

There were three social classes in Irish society, and each corresponded to a similar Indian caste. *Filí* ('poets') were the equivalent of the Brahmin, the *flaith* ('prince', 'noble') was the equivalent of the *Kshatriya* (a warrior aristocracy), and the *aithech* ('farmer' or 'tenant') was the equivalent of the *vaisya*. As already noted, another word for a noble person in Old Irish was *aire*, which corresponds to the Sanskrit *Arya*. *Aire* is still the word we use in Irish today to refer to a government minister.

An old law text further classifies nobles into three classes: *Tri nemid uaisli ... espoc agus flaith agus file* ('Three sacred [esteemed] nobles: bishop, prince, and poet). The word *nemid* has the same roots as the Sanskrit *namas* ('reverence') and is used to refer to a sacred person, place, or thing.

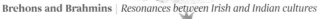

Numbers

B oth Irish and Indian cultures regard certain numbers as having special significance. In Gaelic mythology the numbers five, nine, and twelve were emphasised. There were five provinces, five people in a *geilfine* (the innermost kindred unit), and five lines in the ogham alphabet, which were grouped into five units. The qualities of something or someone were often defined under five headings.

A company of men, on the other hand, was generally considered to have nine members, whether they be the Fianna or explorers setting out to sea. The ninth person or thing was important in divination too, and there were nine doors in Otherworldly buildings.

In contrast, the Indian Vedic tradition does not really highlight these numbers but instead looks to the number two, which represents the duality that exists between God and Nature and also between our senses and our minds, Heaven and Earth, life and death. Seven is also important in Hindu mythology, cosmology, and spirituality, as it represents the seven chakras in the human body and the seven planes of existence. But the most significant number of all in Vedic cosmology, numerology, and ayurvedic medicine is 108. It appears in chants and hymns and on the strings of beads used for meditation. It represents the number of paramours who are single-mindedly devoted to Lord Krishna. This number does not appear to be significant in the Irish tradition, though it is the sum of nine multiplied by twelve, both consequential numbers in Irish mythology.

The one number that could be claimed to have been valued highly by both cultures is seventeen. Cú Chulainn broke seventeen chariots offered to him by a king; Fionn mac Cumhaill had seventeen lovers and was one of seventeen chieftains who commanded the Fianna. The seventeenth of the month is frequently cited in old tales, as is a duration of seventeen days or years. The great adventurer Máel Dúin was advised to sail with seventeen men on the famous voyage on which he encountered an island inhabited by seventeen alluring women.

The Brahmanas are ancient Indian commentaries on the oldest Hindu sacred texts, and in these it is cited that the number of the year is seventeen, as it is made up of twelve months and five seasons. The *Shatapatha Brahmana* (the most important of the Brahamanas) advises that there should be seventeen elements in a sacrifice ritual, as this represents everything. The great Sanskrit epic the *Mahābhārata* has seventeen, plus one, books, in total. I am not completely confident in this latter point, and, in truth, more work would need to be done to claim with any certainty that there are numerological connections between Ireland and India, but it is an intriguing idea.

Carrying

One night during the feast of Samhain, King Ailill and Queen Maeve challenged the bravest of their warriors to tie a wicker band round the ankle of a body of a hanged person that was swinging on a gallows outside the great ceremonial fort at Cruachan. It was a risky venture as the dead were known to roam the land on these specific nights of the year.

A young adventurer named Nera accepted the challenge. He walked out into the pitch darkness and bound a woven band round its ankle. An Otherworldly spirit began to speak from inside the body, begging Nera for a glass of water to quench his thirst. Nera, feeling compassion, took the corpse onto his back and carried it off to fetch a drink for the parched ghost. This gesture of kindness proved foolhardy, as everywhere they went the corpse unleashed a tumult of destruction and death.

Nonetheless, Nera managed to accomplish his task, but when he returned to the fort he discovered that his fellow warriors had been beheaded by an Otherworldly army who were retreating into a deep chasm below the earth. He felt he had no

Corpses

option but to follow them, and once inside the cave he met a fairy woman who warned him that what he had just witnessed was actually a vision of the future. It was a foretelling of a massacre that would occur at the following Samhain feast, if the Otherworldly army had not been defeated by then.

The story is reminiscent of a far older Indian tale, 'The Twenty-Five Stories of the Spectre in the Corpse'. It tells of an Indian king who is asked by a sorcerer, disguised as a beggar, to dare to visit an execution site on the night of a new moon. While there he encounters the body of a hanged man and cuts him down. He carries him on his back through the cremation ground while a ghost inside the corpse tells him stories to shorten the way. When the ghost has shared twenty-five tales with the king, he warns him that the sorcerer plans to kill him to increase his power. He then tells the king how he can outwit this malevolent wizard and obtain his powers for himself. In this way, the king's kindness in caring for the corpse saves his life, just as Nera's life was spared by carrying the corpse outside Cruachan to a source of water. The two stories are different, but they have some alluring parallels.

Brehons and Brahmins | *Resonances between Irish and Indian cultures*

The Blind Man and the Lame Man

The story of Nera carrying the ghost on his back is told in 'Echtra Nerai' ('Adventures of Nera'). Later in the text Nera encounters a blind man with a lame man on his back when he descends into the Otherworld. They are both going to a well, and the blind man asks, 'Is it there?' The lame man replies, 'It is.'

Nera is curious about what they are doing and asks a woman from the Otherworld whom he had married what they are up to. She explains that the blind man is the guardian of the king's crown, which was kept in the well, and that he needs the lame man, who could see, to help him perform his duty. The episode is unrelated to anything else that happened in the story and appears to be a remnant of some far older strand of the tale.

Myles Dillon points out in *Celts and Aryans* that it is reminiscent of a metaphor used to describe the physical and spiritual elements of nature in the school of philosophy known as Samkhya. They are separated into *prakrti* (unintelligent energy), which is equated with being blind, and *purusa* (inert but conscious energy), which is like being crippled. The doctrine of Nyaya (logic) teaches that only by working together can these separate elements accomplish their mission of creation, just as a lame man who can see may reach his destination by mounting on the back of a blind man who can walk.

Brehons and Brahmins | *Resonances between Irish and Indian cultures*

Cattle

The centrality of cattle in Irish and Indian society is remarkable. In many cultures cows represented key components of the mythological, legal, and financial framework, but the extent to which they did so in Ireland and India was exceptional. In Vedic texts and in Bardic Law cattle were regarded as the principal measure of value. Gold only later became the standard in India, while Ireland kept the cow as a unit of currency until early systems of coinage developed after the Norman Conquest. Cattle raids into neighbouring territory for the purpose of winning booty, which the king could then share with his subject, were a regular practice in both lands.

The central story in Irish mythology, *Táin Bó Cuailnge*, is about Queen Maeve's attack on Ulster to steal the Brown Bull of Cooley, while in India the epic Sanskrit poem known as the *Mahabharata* recounts a raid by the Kauravas into the Matsya country of King Virat to carry off his cattle.

Cows
and Rivers

The extraordinary benefits brought about by the domestication of cattle are regularly celebrated in Vedic mythology. The story is told of the initial finding of cows by Sarama and then of the steps taken by Indra and Angi to set them free. The freeing of their milk for human consumption is equated with the freeing of all the rivers by Indra that had been captured by the demon Vritra. Sometimes the two events seem to be combined, and the rivers are thought of as bovine figures that provide water, just as cows provide milk. The Sanskrit for cow, *go*, is found in river names Gomati ('possessing cows') and Godavari ('giving cows').

Irish culture also equated cows with rivers. The Irish for cow, *bó*, is the basis for the name of the River Boyle in Co. Roscommon, and Bó Guaire ('Guaire's cow') is the old name of the Blackwater in Co. Meath.

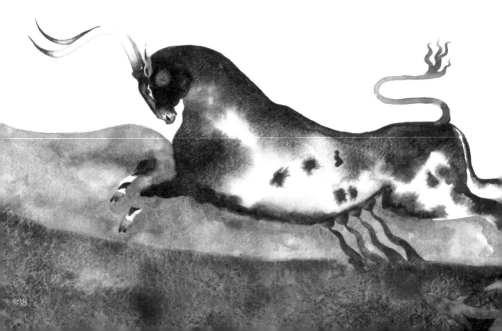

A legend refers to Bó Nemid ('sacred cow') as the name of a river in Ulster. The name of the River Boyne is derived from the name of the mother goddess Bó Finn ('white cow' or 'transparent cow'), who created it from her own limbs. The Boyne is both a cow-like goddess nourishing her people with her endless milk and a river nourishing people with its endless waters.

Bó Finn is closely associated with the Indian god Govinda, an epithet of Krishna, whose name derives from go ('cow') and vinda ('finder of knowledge'). The word *vinda* stems from *uind* ('find out' or 'know'), which is shared by Sanskrit and Celtic languages. It relates to the early Celtic word *vindos* ('white', 'bright' or 'transparent'), as in the name Fionn and the Welsh name Gwynn. Bó Finn therefore refers not only to a white or transparent cow but to one able to see through the veil and access knowledge. Another meaning of Govinda is 'master of the senses'. Cows were considered sacred because they were one of the gateways for the soul to a human body.

The Fosterage of the Houses of the Two Drinking Vessels

The idea that our knowledge of cattle farming and dairy production came from India is suggested in the legend 'The Fosterage of the Houses of the Two Drinking Vessels', which is about how Ethne, the fairest woman in all Ireland, was insulted by Finnbarr, a Tuatha Dé Danann noble, who referred to her as being under the influence of a mysterious figure who sat at her heel. Ethne was so offended by the insinuation that she stopped eating and drinking and would receive sustenance only from two divine cows that she insisted on milking herself into a vessel of gold, using a silken spancel to secure their hind legs. The cows were known as the Dun Cow and the Speckled Cow and were said to have been brought to Ireland from India by two prominent gods of Tuatha Dé Danann, Aengus and Manannán.

These two cows that produced an eternal supply of a healing, nourishing, ambrosia-like milk may be symbols of the wide range of farming techniques and cultural traits brought by early settlers from the East.

King without Blemish

I reland and India share a tradition according to which a king must be entirely without blemish, both physically and morally. The king represents the male energy that unites with the female earth to create a fruitful harvest. Any weakness or disability in them could therefore affect the fertility of the land. This is why in the Hindu epic *Mahabharata* the king of the Kuru Kingdom, Dhritarashtra, could not be monarch because he was blind. Likewise, when the third-century King of Munster, Ailill Ólom, had his ear sliced off he had to surrender his kingship.

Both Irish and Sanskrit tales refer to vigorous kings who brought great prosperity to their people, such as King Rama, during whose reign the trees always bore fruit, the grain flourished, and cattle were free of disease in India. The same is said about the kings Cormac mac Airt and Conchobar mac Nessa in Ireland.

An Ancient Vedic Charm in Ireland

During the first great Tuatha Dé Danann battle in Ireland, their king, Nuada, lost his arm and, being maimed, risked no longer being eligible for kingship. His physician, Dian Céacht, created a prosthetic arm out of silver, but the physician's son Miach claimed he could better his father by reattaching the king's own hand, flesh to flesh. He took the severed limb and uttered a charm that included the words 'Joint to joint of it and sinew to sinew.' Within nine days and nights the joint had healed.

The story survives in a manuscript from the sixteenth century, but it dates to at least the ninth century. It chimes with an account from the same period in which Odin, a god in Germanic mythology, uttered a similar charm while curing a horse: 'Bone to bone, blood to blood, limb to limb, as if they were glued.' Images of Odin healing his horse, as described in the account, date to the fifth or sixth century.

This German account is probably a remnant of Indo-European lore, as the earliest account of the charm is in India, where an oath has been preserved in ancient Vedic texts citing a cure for fractures: 'Thy marrow shall unite with marrow, and thy joint with joint ... and thy bone shall grow together again.'

Most remarkable of all is that this charm was still being used in Ireland into the mid-twentieth century. The Schools Collection of folklore from the late 1930s has numerous accounts of a cure for the sprain in animals that involved saying a version of the words 'Blood to blood and bone to bone and every sinew in its own place.'

Fasting for Debts

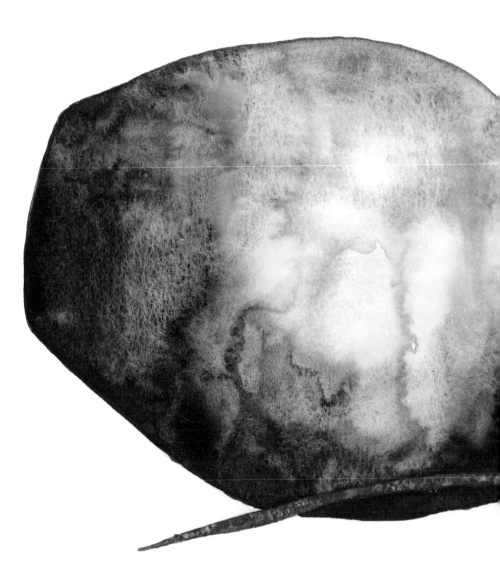

Sanskrit has a word, *prayopavesana*, for the act of someone fasting outside the house of a person who owes them something. It is referred to in India's Lawbook of Manu and even in a far older source from the Vedic period, in which a list of those in whose company one may not eat includes the line 'a creditor who is seated against a debtor, and he who cause him to sit so long.'

This practice of hunger strike to secure justice from someone in debt to you, or more powerful than you, was not common elsewhere, except in Ireland, where, under Brehon Law an individual having a just claim against another person, particularly of higher rank, would undertake a fast at the door of the debtor. After a reasonable period, if the claim was not satisfied, the fasting claimant would be entitled to seize the property of the debtor in an amount equal to twice the value of the original claim. If the claimant was injured or had died, the debtor would be held liable.

This corresponds to another Indian account of the practice of *dharna*, by which the creditor, especially if he was a Brahmin, fasted in front of the debtor's house until he yielded. If he died the debtor was responsible for the Brahmin's death. It's no coincidence that many of the most well-known hunger strikers are Irish and Indian: Mahatma Gandhi, Terence MacSwiney, and Bobby Sands.

Marrowbones and Butter-Cakes

C hristy Moore sings a song called 'Tippin' It up to Nancy' that goes:

With me right finnickineerio, me tip finnick a wall
With me right finnickineerio, we're tipping it up to Nancy.

He learnt the song from the Co. Roscommon Traveller singer John Reilly. It tells of an unfaithful wife who asks the chemist how to make her husband blind so that he won't know what's going on. The chemist says:

Give him eggs and marrowbones and make him suck them all,
Before he has the last one sucked, he won't see you at all.

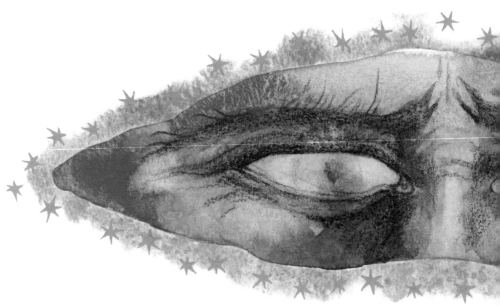

Sure enough, the husband goes blind and says he'll drown himself in the river. His wife offers to show him the way, but he pushes her in instead.

It sounds like a classic Irish folk song, but it derives from an ancient Indian collection of interrelated animal fables known as the Panchatantra ('Five Treatises'). These Sanskrit tales date to well over two thousand years ago. In one of them, 'The Butter-Blinded Brahmin', an account is given of an unfaithful wife who asks the statue of a goddess at a river how to blind her husband. By way of reply she hears the words, 'If you never stop giving him such food as butter and butter-cakes, then he will presently go blind.' She does as advised, and her husband appears to go blind, but he tricks her and instead kills her lover and cuts off her nose.

Strawboys and Gandharvas

There was a tradition in Ireland of young men disguised in straw masks and elaborate headdresses turning up uninvited at a wedding or a bride's house to sing and dance to ensure good fortune and health for the couple. In return, drinks and gifts would be bestowed on them. The origins of the tradition are uncertain, but it probably stems from an old pagan ritual surrounding fertility and fortune.

The straw boys bear a certain similarity to semi-divine, celestial creatures known as gandharvas in Hinduism and Buddhism. These half-man, half-bird beings are known for their musical and dancing ability. They too are considered vital at weddings for ensuring fertility in the marriage. In fact, the Buddha explains that for an embryo to fertilise and develop, a woman must be in the correct point of her menstrual cycle, she must have intercourse with a man, and a gandharva must be present when they come together.

Aengus and the Apsara Nymph

In Hindu and Buddhist mythology, apsaras are female spirits, a bit like nymphs or fairies, who occupy the clouds and waters. They love to dance and are often paired with gandharvas, who play beautiful spirit music for them. There was an apsara named Urvashi in India long ago who married a king, Pururavas, on condition that he hugged her three times each day and never let her see him naked. The gandharvas were upset that she had fallen for a human, and through some dastardly conniving they managed to lure her back to them, and she abandoned the king.

Pururavas was left bereft. He embarked on a long journey to find her and win her back. After much searching, he caught sight of her flying over a lake amid a flock of swans. He called out to her, imploring her to return to him. Out of pity, she agreed to see him one more time, on the last day of the year. He knew this could never be enough to satisfy him, and so he began to mull over a way to be with her forever. He settled on the idea of asking the gandharva spirits to transform him into one of them so that he could be with her forever more, without incurring their wrath. They agreed, and Urvashi and Pururavas were reunited.

In the Irish tradition, 'The Dream of Aengus' relates a similar story of how Aengus, son of the great gods Dagda and Boann, became besotted with a beautiful woman who appeared to him repeatedly in dreams playing alluring music. He was so haunted by her beauty that he realised he would have to track her down in this earthly dimension. Like the Indian king, he embarked on a long journey to find her, and after much searching he too spotted her, eventually, among a large flock of swans over a lake. He wondered how he could ever be with her.

He sought out the advice of the greatest minds, who could tell him only that at Samhain every other year she transformed herself into a bird and would return to the physical world. One elder advised him that if he went to the lake on the evening between the last day of the old year and first day of the new one, he might encounter her and could try to convince her to remain with him.

Aengus did as instructed, and when his beloved appeared he begged her to approach him. She hesitantly came forward and allowed him to hug her. Once his arms were round her he began to transform into a bird himself. They were able to be intimate together, and then they both flew up into the sky and away off to the fairy realm. From that point on, Aengus has always been associated with love in the old tales, just as the apsaras and gandharvas are still associated with love in India today.

Expanding Cloaks and Saris

The Irish saint and pagan goddess Brigid gets her name from the Proto-Celtic word *briganti* ('high' or 'exalted'). In the *Rigveda*, the oldest known Vedic Sanskrit text and one of the four sacred canonical texts of Hinduism, the Goddess of the Dawn, Ushas, is referred to as *Brhati*, an epithet meaning 'Her Highness' or 'Exalted One'—the same word from the same Indo-European root.

The best-known story about Brigid is about how the King of Leinster refused to give her enough land to establish a settlement until she convinced him that all she wanted was the extent of ground that could be covered by the cloak on her back. The king relented and she laid down her cloak, whereupon it magically extended to cover a vast swathe of Co. Kildare.

The incident is vaguely reminiscent of what happened to Draupadi, the principal female character in the *Mahābhārata*, when her five husbands lost her to the Kaurava brothers in a gambling game. She tried to protest against the legality and morality of the bet, but she was rebutted and told to strip, as she was now a slave. Her sari was pulled from her in a crowded assembly hall, but Lord Krishna intervened, extending the garment indefinitely so that, no matter how much her oppressors pulled, she remained clothed. Ultimately, her meagre piece of cotton defeated and humiliated her enemies.

Kings and Horse Baths

I n the thirteenth century the chronicler Gerald of Wales wrote an account of Ireland in which he described a king in Donegal copulating with a white mare and then killing it as part of an inauguration ritual. The horse was then boiled in a cauldron in which the king bathed, and he then ate the horseflesh and drank the cauldron broth. Gerald's description of Ireland is often fanciful, but this account does appear to be a partly accurate recreation of an ancient pagan fertility rite in which the land is represented by the mare. A legend about the seventh-century St Moling seems to refer to this ritual when the saint is offered a cauldron of horseflesh from which to eat and drink.

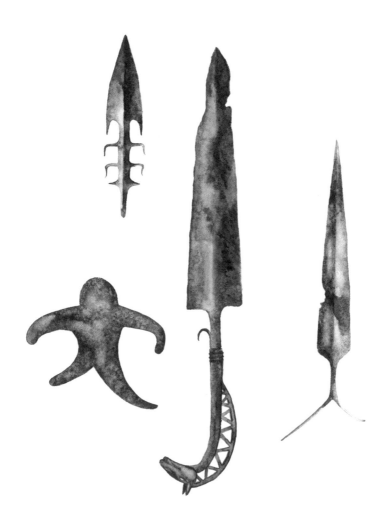

In ancient India this concept had a name, *ashvamedha*, which refers to the sacrifice of a stallion at the inauguration of a king. It was one of the grandest of the Vedic religious rites and is recorded in numerous texts, including the *Shatapatha Brahmana*. The ceremony was incredibly complex, with many stages that took a year and hundreds of people to complete. At its culmination the king and horse were bathed and then the horse was suffocated, after which the queen lay down and pretended to have intercourse with it. It was then dismembered and used in sacrificial offerings. The practice was condemned by the Buddha in the fifth or sixth century BC but continued for centuries, possibly into the eleventh century.

Horse Urine and Chariots

According to legend, both Lough Ree and Lough Neagh in Ireland were formed by the continuous stream of urine from a magical horse. There is a parallel reference in the *Rigveda* that states that deities known as the Maruts ride through the sky in chariots drawn by stallions whose urine falls as rain. 'Send down for us the rain of heaven, ye Maruts, and let the Stallion's flood descend in torrents.'

It is noteworthy that the Maruts drive chariots rather than ride horses. In Indian and Celtic tradition, kings and gods tended also to drive rather than ride. The great Celtic god Mananánn mac Lir travels in a chariot of white horses, and Cú Chulainn goes into battle driven by Loeg, his charioteer. The other two most prominent heroes, Conall Cernach and Lóegaire Búadach, are also chariot-fighters. In India, at the *rajasuya* (consecration of a king), the king drives in a chariot and makes a mock cattle raid. In the *Mahābhārata*, Krishna acts as Arjuna's charioteer.

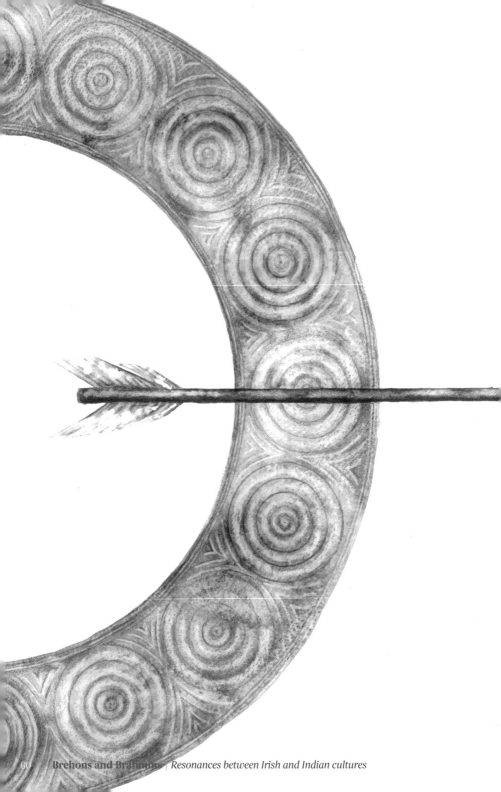

Buddha and Bua

The spiritual tradition of Buddhism began when Siddhartha Gautama attained enlightenment while meditating under the Bodhi tree in Bodh Gaya in India. He was referred to as the Buddha, which derives from the past participle of the stem *budh* ('to know', 'to awaken', or 'to be enlightened'). In the Vedas the planet Mercury is also known as *budh*. Interestingly, an Irish manuscript from the ninth century kept in Würzburg defines the Old Irish word *budh* as 'point of fire' and 'planet Mercury'. The tenth-century Sanas Cormaic ('Cormac's Glossary') translates *budh/bott* as 'Áine's fire'. Áine was an Irish deity connected with brightness or sun. Might this hint at some crossover between Celtic and Vedic astrology?

The Sanskrit *budh* stems from the Indo-European word *bud*, 'to awake'. It is similar to the Irish word *bua* ('to win'), from the Old Irish *búaid* ('winning', 'victorious', 'accomplished', 'exulted') and is at the root of the name Boudicca, the Celtic warrior queen.

Similarly, the word for fairy or sorceress in Sanskrit, *siddhayogini*, derives from the root *siddha* ('perfected') and can refer to someone who has achieved a high degree of physical and spiritual development. It shares a linguistic root with the Old Irish *sidhe*, a fairy or fairy mound, which suggests that the *síoga* ('fairies', 'Otherworldly beings') may have represented much more than we give them credit for now. They are nature entities or beings of enlightenment in the landscape who try to widen our horizons and expand our minds beyond the mundane. Interestingly, many fairy stories focus on their revelling in an abundance of vibrancy, joy, and health, as they continually feast, dance, play music, and enjoy the sensory pleasures of life, without worrying about limitations or hardship.

Five Provinces

The word for a province in Irish is *cúige* (from Old Irish *cóiced*, 'a fifth'), although there are only four of them: Ulster, Leinster, Munster, and Connacht. The fifth one was at the very centre, unifying them. Some say it was invisible or was in another realm at the point at which the four provinces connected with the Otherworld. It was called Mide ('middle'). The Brahmanas also describe the regions of India as east, south, west, north, and centre. The Sanskrit word *madhya* is used for 'middle' and has the same linguistic root as *mide*.

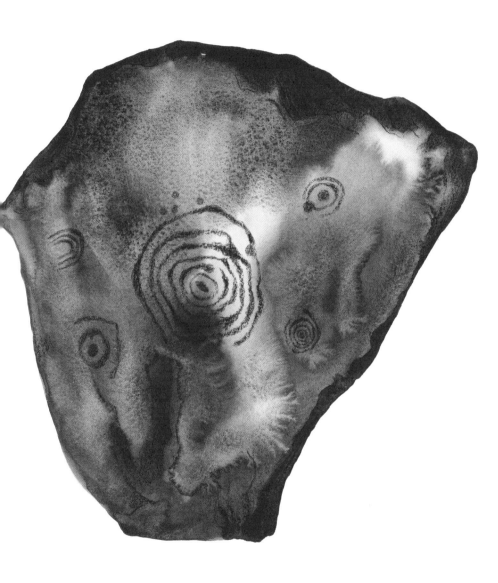

Poetry and Prose

Many Irish stories and legends are thousands of years old. They were passed down from mouth to mouth by *seanchaithe* ('storytellers') until they were written down when writing came to Ireland with the arrival of Christianity in the fifth century. The stories preserved in old manuscripts have sections of prose interspersed with occasional passages of verse or dialogue to mark any heightening of emotion. While the prose parts were flexible and left to the creative memory of the individual *seanchaí*, the verse sections remained constant and had to be repeated exactly as they were passed down through time. They were often in a more archaic form of Irish.

A similar combination of prose and verse can be found in the *Rigveda*, the Vedic Brahmanas, and the Buddhist Jatakas (stories of past lives of the Buddha on his journey to enlightenment). In these, too, the verse parts are often far older than the prose.

The verse sections of the Brahmanas and the *Mahābhārata* were possibly sung or at least chanted, and this practice remained alive with the *akhyana* (stories narrated in musical form right into the 1970s and even up to today). It is thought that verse sections of some Irish sagas were also sung or chanted. The language of these passages is often obscure and is for the most part still untranslated. It is written in an archaic metre, with alliteration but no rhyme, and a varying number of syllables in each line, as though it dates to an earlier era.

In 'The Death of the Sons of Uisneach', a druid foretells the birth of Deirdre in verse, and her lament and her speech in defiance of the king may also have been sung. Likewise, 'The Voyage of Bran' contains two long poems recounting the invitation to Bran to travel and the welcome he receives from the god Manannán. These poems make up more than half the text. It is possible that they were sung as the *akhyana* still are in Gujarat today.

The King and the Commoner

There are motifs and storylines common to Irish and Indian sagas. One involves a girl of non-noble lineage being spotted in the woods by a king who then becomes besotted by her and determined to marry her against the wishes of court officials. The *Mahābhārata* tells the story of Shakuntala, a humble foster-child of the hermit Kanya who had no royal blood or connection to nobility. One day King Dushyanta was hunting deer by chariot in the forests in northern India and spotted Shakuntala watering the sacred trees at her foster-father's hermitage. The king was smitten by her beauty, modesty, and timidity. She too was entranced by him, and they married, though soon after she was cursed by a *rishi* ('seer' or 'druid') who wiped all memory of her from Dushyanta's mind. Fortunately, the spell was broken and the loving couple led a happy life with many children, one of whom was Bharata, whose descendants were the Kauravas and Pandavas, two rival groups of cousins whose endless conflict is a central theme of the *Mahābhārata*.

The twelfth-century manuscript The Book of Leinster contains a somewhat similar story called 'The Music of Buchet's House', which is about the adventures of the innkeeper Buchet, who retires to a small hut in the forest near Kells, just like the hermit in India, to escape the injustices and travails of the world. His foster-child is named Eithne, and one day while she in the woods doling out portions of rushes, water, and milk she is spotted by Cormac mac Airt, a powerful leader who will soon become king. He falls in love with her and determines to marry her against all the advice of his courtiers. They too marry, and their marriage leads to endless complications for themselves and others. In truth, this is just another example of a story about a king marrying a commoner, a popular motif throughout the world, right up to Prince Charles marrying Lady Diana Spencer in the 1980s.

The Sea Is Held Back by a Tool

In Indian lore Parashurama, an incarnation of the god Vishnu, was offered as much of the sea as he could encompass by a throw of his axe. He stood on a promontory and hurled his axe southwards, and the ocean receded from the space within the throw, yielding the Malabar coast as his kingdom. In the Dindshenchas, the Irish lore of placenames, Tuirbe Trágmar threw his axe against the flowing tide, and the tide was held back and could advance no further.

One of the possibilities for the migration from India westwards was when Parasurama was engaging in the killing of the ksatriya classes (which he did 21 times). The Celts (Daityas and Dandavas) could be the migration of the ksatriya armies.

Celtic Gods and Yogic Gurus

On first appearance, traditional Irish and Indian art and decoration seem very different, and yet there are similarities to be found between certain examples of Celtic carvings and ancient Indian images. For example, a Celtic deity, Cernunnos, a horned god of fertility, is frequently depicted sitting in lotus position with an Indian-style headdress and meditative gaze. He looks uncannily like depictions of the Indian god Shiva, and there are other carvings of Celtic sages posed in meditative postures, like a yoga guru.

Old Irish and

The linguistic similarities between Irish and Indian languages such as Hindi, Bengali, and Punjabi are accepted by scholars and most likely arose from their common linguistic ancestor, Proto-Indo European. The most widespread hypothesis holds that this early mother language was spoken by farmers living in the Pontic steppe, north of the Black Sea, in the fourth millennium BC. As people spread out, the language evolved into different language families, such as Celtic languages, Indo-Iranian, Hellenic, Balto-Slavic and Germanic. Most European and West Asian languages stem from this same root, but migration patterns and cultural exchanges caused them to adapt and evolve so much since then that it can be hard to see what once united them.

Irish and Sanskrit (and the modern Indian languages that stem from Sanskrit, such as Hindi) have retained a remarkable number of similar words and grammatical constructions, possibly because they were able to conserve old qualities for longer as a result of their history and location. Words that appear to be shared include the Irish word *aire* (which refers to 'nobles', the highest caste in Ireland) and the Sanskrit word *aryas* ('noblemen' in North Indian society), and *naib*, a Sanskrit word for 'good', which is from the same ancestral root as the Old Irish word *noeib*, from which the modern Irish word *naomh* ('saint') derives.

Sanskrit

Other parallel words include the Sanskrit *badhira* ('deaf'), which is *bodhar* in Irish, and the Sanskrit *udaka* ('water'), which is uisce in Irish. The Sanskrit *trasa* ('to cross') is *trasna* in Irish. *Āhāra* ('to eat') is *itheadh* in Irish. Balacha ('boy' in Bengali and Hindi) is buachail in Irish. Even the present tense of the copula (a word that connects the subject and predicate in a sentence) is remarkably similar in both languages: In Irish it is conjugated as *Is mé, is tú, is é / is í, is sinn, is sibh*, and *s'iad*, and in Sanskrit it is *Asmi, Asi, Asti, Smah, Stha*, and *Santi*.

There are many other features that show remarkable commonality, such as aspiration, in which consonants are occasionally pronounced with an accompanying forceful expulsion of air, and nasalization, whereby a sound is pronounced by allowing air to escape through the nose at the same time as it flows through the mouth. In fact, Prof. Calvert Watkins of Harvard University believed that the structure of Old Irish (the version of the languages spoken in Ireland from the seventh to the tenth century and that is still somewhat comprehensible to Irish speakers today) is most closely related to Vedic Sanskrit.

These linguistic connections are certainly not clearcut, but they do serve to remind us of the intricate web of human interaction and exchange. They are a testament to the enduring quest for communication, expression, and the preservation of ideas, transcending time and borders.

Conclusion

So, what should we make of all these parallels and similarities in the tales, beliefs, laws, and traditional practices of two cultures separated by an entire continent? The echoes and resonances between them appear noteworthy. Individually, each could be dismissed as a coincidence, but taken together they suggest something more: some underlying connection that deserves further exploration. This connection suggests that the roots of Irish culture are deeper and wider than might first appear and that our people and culture stem from something more ancient than we might imagine.

It is fair to say that within the relatively limited span of recorded history (which in Ireland dates to the arrival of written texts with the introduction of Christianity) there has not been enough interaction between Ireland and the Indian subcontinent for such a crossover of ideas

and expressions of culture. In fact, there has been virtually no connection until the second half of the nineteenth century, when some Irish people were posted to India to serve in the colonial administration and the military during the height of the British Raj.

The only logical explanation, therefore, is that the links stem from before the era of recorded history, from a time when early settled communities were encountering each other in the expanses of eastern Europe and western Asia while developing the techniques of cattle farming, dairy production, and grain growing that allowed the people of these Indo-European cultures to advance and prosper.

None of these insights is in any way new. They have been documented and generally accepted among scholars for well over a century, but our culture was so fixated on the New World and on gazing westwards towards the future that we tended to overlook them.

Our recognition of these connections was also paralysed by the fact that the Nazis purposely misinterpreted Indo-European cultural links to bolster their policies of racism and genocide. As mentioned in the introduction, their deceitful claims about an elite European race descended from India have been fully and finally rejected—as must the more recent attempts by right-wing Hindu nationalists to skew their history at the expense of Indian Muslims. The best way to ensure this, I believe, is to acknowledge and celebrate Ireland's surprising, but genuine, links to the lore and language of the Indian subcontinent in an honourable and honest way.

At this time, when populations are once again moving in search of new opportunities and when wars and climate change are sparking mass migration, it is especially important to acknowledge that we in Ireland, too, were once migrants: we came here from somewhere else. It is therefore fitting that we should look back and track the directions in which we have branched since that communal era of our tentative beginnings millennia ago.

Acknowledgements

Sincere thanks to Joshue O'Connor for reading through multiple drafts and offering great insights and leads. My thanks also to Jonny Dillon, David McDonnell, Jayee Borcar, Ruairí Ó Brógáin, Antic Ham, Paul Whelan, Sarah Fox, Anna Tanvir and Maninder Singh, Colm Mac Con Iomara, Nadasen Genasen Pillay, and Dónal Ó Céilleachair for offering guidance and support.

Also, to all the people on Instagram, Facebook, Twitter, and Tiktok who offered suggestions and opinions regarding the title of this book. I agree with so many of you who said that *Celtic Karma*, *Dúchas & Dharma*, *Delhi to Derry*, etc were all great potential names for the book.

And to the late Professor Daithí Ó hÓgáin of the Folklore Department of UCD who handed me a book of Vedic texts in 1996 as I was about to embark on my first journey through India, and told me to keep an eye and ear out for cultural similarities I might encounter along the way. The word he used was a 'dekko', a slang for 'look' that was brought back by British and Irish soldiers stationed in India in the 19th century. He told me it was from the Hindi *dekho*, and wondered if it might be related to the Irish *d'fhéach* ('look').

- *Manchán*

I would like to thank Paul, Sylvie, Meaghan and Claire for their unceasing support, and Ceci, Ashley, Nichole, Trasan, Dónal, Aaron, Chrissie, and Aidan for every suggestion and spontaneous brainstorming session.

- *Aurélie*

About the author

Manchán Magan

Manchán has written books on his travels in Africa, India and South America. He writes occasionally for *The Irish Times,* and presents the Almanac of Ireland podcast for RTÉ. He has made dozens of documentaries on issues of world culture for TG4, RTÉ, and the Travel Channel. His books include *Thirty-Two Words For Field, Listen to the Land Speak, Tree Dogs, Banshee Fingers and Other Irish Words For Nature,* and *Wolf-Men and Water Hounds.* With Antic-Ham, he's collaborated on two art books for Redfoxpress.

www.manchan.com

About the illustrator

Aurélie Beatley

Aurélie is a Franco-American illustrator and animator based in Scotland who specialises in folklore, mythology, and endangered languages. She has created work for the Smithsonian Institution, *National Geographic*, the International Monetary Fund, and Public Radio International.

www.aureliebeatley.com

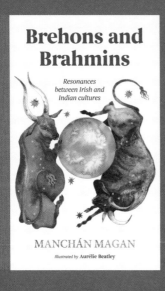

Brehons and Brahmins is the first in a trilogy Manchán will be publishing with Mayo Books Press.

It will soon be followed by illustrated books exploring cultural similarities and resonances between Ireland and Iceland, and Ireland and the Aboriginal cultures of Australia.

Manchán's previous works for Mayo Books Press:

Focail na mBan is a gathering of Irish words for vaginas, vulvas, clitorises and periods with illustrations from 29 artists.

It is meant as a catalyst for those willing to seek out further terms and insights from older lore-keepers in the Gaeltacht. This humble first step is a gesture of encouragement for others who may wish to dive deeper into this rich realm of linguistic insight. It is illustrated with the works of 29 artists who responded to the words.

Also included are articles by poet, Annemarie Ní Churreáin; writer, Tadhg Mac Eoghain; and some poetry by Dairena Ní Chinnéide.